Così fan Tutte

Comic Opera in two Acts by
Wolfgang Amadeus Mozart

Words by Lorenzo da Ponte

English Version by David Higham

Vocal Score by Arthur Willner

Price **17/6** *net*
(1954)
CURRENT PRICE
19/6 NETT
BOOSEY & HAWKES LTD.

———————

Boosey & Co.
Limited
Sole Selling Agents :
Boosey & Hawkes Ltd.
295 Regent Street, London W.1
Paris · Bonn · Capetown · Sydney · Toronto · New York

Printed in England

Characters

(in the order of their appearance)

Ferrando ⎱	... ...	*Tenor*
Guglielmo ⎰ *Officers*	... ...	*Bass*
Don Alfonso, *an elderly philosopher* ...	...	*Baritone*
Fiordiligi ⎱	... ...	*Soprano*
Dorabella ⎰ *Sisters*	... ...	*Mezzo-Soprano*
Despina, *servant to the sisters*	... ...	*Soprano*

Chorus of Soldiers, Townspeople, Singers, Musicians and Servants.
The scene is laid in Naples.

INDEX

B. & H. 16562

Act II

Scene 1

In addition to the grace-notes which Mozart himself wrote down in the vocal parts it has been customary to sing many additional appoggiaturas, especially in recitatives, following the Italian convention which dates back to long before the days of Mozart. These appoggiaturas have not been printed in the present score because they have always been traditionally left to the discretion of the singers. No hard and fast rule can be laid down for their performance, but in most cases where a descending phrase has a feminine ending, i.e., with an accented penultimate syllable followed by a final syllable on a weak beat, both being given the same musical note, the strong beat should be treated as an appoggiatura and sung to the note one degree above that actually written, so that the cadence falls by a tone or semitone to the final note.

Examples:

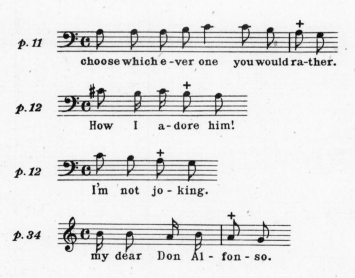

COSÌ FAN TUTTE
Overture

W. A. MOZART

Cosi fan tutte

3

Così fan tutte

ACT I

SCENE 1. A Café

Nº 1. Terzetto

Cosi fan tutte

B. & H. 16562

Cosi fan tutte

Così fan tutte

Fer. -plain to us just why you think our mis-tress-es are like-ly to at-tempt to de-
su - bi - to, per-chè d'in - fe - del - tà le no-stre a-man-ti so-spet-ta - te ca-

Fer. - ceive us. I tell you stop your
- pa - ci. Ces - sa - te di scher-

Don Alfonso
Oh, what a sim-ple soul! How I a-dore him!
Ca - ra sem-pli - ci - tà, quan-to mi pia - ci!

Fer. jokes, or else, by heaven...
- zar, o giu-ro al cie-lo—

A. And I, swearing by this world, tell you that I'm not joking.
Ed io, giu-ro al-la ter-ra, non scherzo, a-mi-ci mi-ei:

A. All that I want to know is what spe-cial type of creature are these your charming ladies. Have
so - lo sa-per vor-re - i che raz-za d'a-ni-ma-li son que-ste vo-stre bel-le, se han

B. & H. 16562

Cosi fan tutte

B. & H. 16562

№ 2. Terzetto

Don Alfonso *scherzando*

Like the Phoenix of my-tho-lo-gy, Constant wo-men lie be-fore us. They ex-
È la fe-de del-le fem-mi-ne co-me l'a-ra-ba Fe-ni-ce: che vi

A. -ist, so sings the cho-rus, so sings the cho-rus; Where they
sia cias-cun lo di-ce, cias-cun lo di-ce; do-ve

A. are, though, where they are, though, no
si-a, do-ve si-a, nes-

A. man can say. **Ferrando** *con fuoco* Phoe-nix! That's my Do-ra-bel-la!
-sun lo sa. La Fe-ni-ce è Do-ra-bel-la!

Guglielmo *con fuoco* Phoe-nix! That's my Fior-di-
La Fe-ni-ce è Fior-di-

Così fan tutte

B.& H. 16562

16

Cosi fan tutte

B. & H. 16562

Così fan tutte   B. & H. 16562

Cosi fan tutte

20

Cosi fan tutte

B. & H. 16562

№ 3. Terzetto

B.& H. 16562

22

Cosi fan tutte

Così fan tutte

Cosi fan tutte

SCENE 2. A garden by the seashore. Fiordiligi and Dorabella each looking at a miniature.

Nọ 4. Duet

Andante *dolce.*

Fiordiligi

Ah, sis-ter, my dear-est, ah, sis-ter, my dear-est,
Ah, guar-da, so-rel-la, ah, guar-da, so-rel-la,

Fio.

Sis - ter! Sis - ter; his gaze is the clear-est, His
guar-da! guar-da, se boc-ca più bel-la, se a-

Fio.

lips far more beau-ti-ful than e'er.... man could claim,............ than
-spet-to più no-bi-le si può.... ri-tro-var,............ si

28

Cosi fan tutte

Così fan tutte

RECIT.
Fiordiligi

It seems to me this morn-ing ev-'ry vein, ev-'ry ar-te-ry is ting-ling. If I could
Mi par, che stammat-ti-na vo-lon-tie-ri fa-rei la paz-za-rel-la: ho un cer-to

32

Cosi fan tutte

B. & H. 16562

SCENE 3. (Enter Don Alfonso)

№ 5. Aria

Allegro agitato

A. mas-ter! / fa-to! | When I speak, my lips are dry, my lips are / Vor-rei dir, e cor non ho, e cor non

A. dry. How I stam-mer, my words are few! And how- / ho bal - bet - tan-do il lab - bro va fuor la

A. -ev- er hard I try, Still my voice will not come through. / vo-ce u-scir non può, ma mi re - sta mez - za quà.

A. What will you do? What shall I? Oh, I can't believe it's / Che fa - re - te? Che fa - rò? Oh, che gran fa-ta - li-

A. true! It's e-nough to make you cry, to make you cry. How I / tà! Dar di peg-gio non si può, ah non si può, oh di

A.

grieve   for   them,   for   you, how   I   grieve   for
voi,   di   lor   for   pie   tà,   oh   di   voi,   for   di

cresc.   p

A.

them,   for   you, how   I   grieve   for   them,   for
lor   for   pie   tà,   oh   di   voi,   di   lor   pie -

cresc.   p

A.

you,   for   them, for   you,   for   them,   for   you.
- tà,   di   lor   pie - tà,   di   lor   pie - tà.

RECIT.
Fiordiligi

Mer - cy!   For good-ness sake, dear Don Al - fon - so,   don't tor-ment   us   like
Stel - le!   Per ca - ri - tà, Si - gnor Al - fon - so,   non ci fa - te   mo -

Fio.

this!
- rir.

Dorabella

Oh heavens! What e - vil's come upon us
Oh De - i!   Qual ma-le è ad-di-ve-nu-to

Don Alfonso

First, I must warn you, you will need all your courage.
Convien ar-mar-vi, fi-glie mie, di co-stan-za.

Così fan tutte

Così fan tutte

B. & H. 16562

Cosi fan tutte

SCENE 4. Enter Ferrando and Guglielmo in uniform.

Nº 6. Quintet

40

Cosi fan tutte

B. & H. 16562

Così fan tutte

B.& H. 16562

Cosi fan tutte

B. & H. 16562

Così fan tutte

Così fan tutte

№ 7. Duettino

Così fan tutte

SCENE 5. A boat arrives at the shore. During the following March, a troop of soldiers enters, accompan-
-ied by a crowd of townspeople.

Nº 8. Chorus

Maestoso

CHORUS

SOPRANO
ALTO

Oh, the sol-dier's life for me! Oh, the sol-dier's life for me! Here to-
Bel-la vi - ta mi - li - tar, bel-la vi - ta mi - li - tar! O - gni

TENOR

BASS

S.
A.

- day and gone to-mor-row, Quaffing joy, then sip-ping sor-row, Now on land and now on
di si can-gia lo - co, og - gi mol - to, do-man po - co, o-ra in ter-ra,ed or sul

T.
B.

Cosi fan tutte

Nº 9. Quintet

A.
-tal-ion's de-part-ed. But you can ov-er-haul it with your mess-mates, who are
-ti-ta la bar-ca, rag-giun-ger-la con-vien con poc-chi a-mi-ci che su
Fiordiligi
My heart is
Muo-jo d'af-
Dorabella
My heart is
Muo-jo d'af-
Ferrando
Then hold me tight, my darling.
Ab-brac-cia-mi, i-dol mi-o!
A.
here with the pinnace, which is yours for the taking.
le-gno più lie-ve at-ten-den-do vi stanno.
Guglielmo
Then hold me tight, my darling.
Ab-brac-cia-mi, i-dol mi-o!

Nº 9. Quintet

Fio.
(weeping.)
breaking. You'll write me ev-'ry morn-ing,
-fan-no! Di scri-ver-mi o-gni gior-no,
Dor.
(weeping.)
breaking. You'll write me twice a
-fan-no! Due vol-te an-co-ra
G.
Be
Non
Andante
p

58

Così fan tutte

Flo. / Dor. / Fer. / G.
- dieu,.... love. A - dieu, love.
- di - o! ad - di - - o!

A.
laughter, I'll burst myself with laughter, laughter, laughter, laughter, laughter.
ri - do, io cre - po, se non ri - do, se non ri - do, se non ri - do.

During the repetition of the Chorus, Ferrando and Guglielmo enter the boat, which then leaves the landing place. The soldiers march off, the people follow them.

CHORUS

SOPRANO / ALTO
Oh, the sol - dier's life for me, Oh, the sol - dier's life for me! Here to-
Bel - la vi - ta mi - li - tar, bel - la vi - ta mi - li - tar! O - gni

TENOR / BASS
Maestoso

S. A.
- day and gone to - mor - row, Quaffing joy, then sip - ping sor - row, Now on
di si can - gia lo - co, og - gi mol - to, do - man po - co, or - a in

T. B.

Cosi fan tutte   B. & H. 16562

62

Cosi fan tutte

B. & H. 16562

SCENE 6

Cosi fan tutte

Cosi fan tutte

Così fan tutte

RECIT.
Don Alfonso

A pret-ty lit-tle co - me-dy! The next thing— a ren-dez-vous with
Non son cat-ti-vo co-mi-co! va be-ne— al con-cer - ta-to

these my two dis-ci-ples of the sword and the so-fa. They'll be there pret-ty
lo-co i due cam-pio-ni di Ci-pri-gna e di Mar-te mi sta-ran-no at-ten-

soon now. I'll go and find them— I mustn't keep them wait-ing. What gri-
-den-do; or sen-za in-du-gio, rag-giun-ger-li con-vie-ne. Quan-te

-ma-ces! Oh what a cage of mon-keys! All the bet-ter for me: they'll tum-ble all the
smor-fie, quan-te buf-fo-ne-ri-e! Tan-to me-glio per me, ca-dran più fa-cil-

fas-ter. These ex-tra-va-gant creatures are the first ones to be turned top-sy-
-men-te: que-sta raz-za di gente è la più pre-sta a can-giar-si d'u-

-tur-vy. Oh, sil-ly as-ses, to lose a hun-dred each bet-ting on
-mo-re. Oh po-ve-ri-ni! per fe-mmi-na gio-car cen-to zec-

las-ses! To make a po-tion,
-chi-ni! Nel ma-re sol-ca,

Allegro moderato

Who tries to squeeze a le-mon in God's migh-ty o-cean
e nell' a-re-na se-mi-na, e il va-go ven-to

Has as much of sense as he Who lays his
spe-ra in re-te ac-co-glie-re chi fon-da

(Exit)

hope of hea-ven on bo-som fe-mi-nine.
sue spe-ran-ze in cor di fe-mmi-na.

Così fan tutte

B.&H. 16562

SCENE 8. A room with tables and chairs, etc. Three doors, two at sides and one in background. Despina preparing a drink of chocolate.

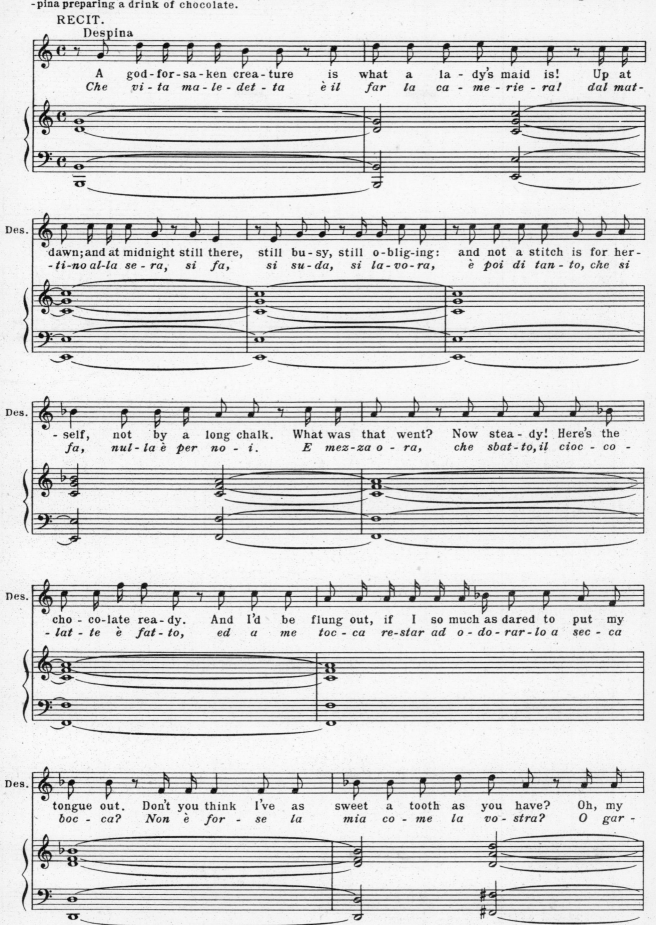

RECIT.

Despina

A god-for-sa-ken crea-ture is what a la-dy's maid is! Up at
Che vi-ta ma-le-det-ta è il far la ca-me-rie-ra! dal mat-

dawn; and at midnight still there, still bu-sy, still o-blig-ing: and not a stitch is for her-
-ti-no al-la se-ra, si fa, si su-da, si la-vo-ra, è poi di tan-to, che si

-self, not by a long chalk. What was that went? Now stea-dy! Here's the
fa, nul-la è per no-i. E mez-za o-ra, che sbat-to, il cioc-co-

cho-co-late rea-dy. And I'd be flung out, if I so much as dared to put my
-lat-te è fat-to, ed a me toc-ca re-star ad o-do-rar-lo a sec-ca

tongue out. Don't you think I've as sweet a tooth as you have? Oh, my
boc-ca? Non è for-se la mia co-me la vo-stra? O gar-

Così fan tutte

B. & H. 16562

Des. dear Mis-ses Muf-fet, why should I on-ly sniff it, while you can stuff it? My
-ba-te Si-gno-re, che a voi des-si l'es-sen-za ea me l'o-do-re? per

(wiping her mouth)

Des. word, I'm going to taste it. Oo, it's love-ly! They're coming! Oh Lord, ne-ver a warning.
Bac-co, vo'as-sa-giar-lo: com'è buo-no! Vien gen-te! oh ciel! son le pa-dro-ne.

SCENE 9

Enter Fiordiligi and Dorabella

Des. My la-dies, will you take cho-co-late this morning? Ji - mi-ni! What's the trouble?
Ma-da-me, ec - co la vo-stra col-la-zio-ne. Dia-mi-ne! co-sa fa-te?

Fiordiligi

Ah! I want a dag-ger— or some poi-son would do.
Ah! Ov'è un ac-cia-ro? un ve-le-no, dov' è?

Dorabella

Ah!
Ah!

Des. Why, what's the mat-ter? My
Che co-sa è na-to? Pa-

Cosi fan tutte

74

Nº 11. Aria

Cosi fan tutte

B. & H. 16562

Cosi fan tutte

Così fan tutte

78

Cosi fan tutte

B. & H. 16562

Cosi fan tutte

B. & H. 16562

Cosi fan tutte

Così fan tutte

Cosí fan tutte

№ 12. Aria

Così fan tutte

86

Così fan tutte   B. & H. 16562

Cosi fan tutte

88.

SCENE 10

Cosi fan tutte

Despina

Cosi fan tutte

Cosi fan tutte

B & H 165

SCENE 11

Nº 13. Sextet

97

Cosi fan tutte

B.& H. 16562

98

Cosi fan tutte

B.& H. 16562

Cosi fan tutte

Cosi fan tutte

B. & H. 16562

Così fan tutte

B. & H. 16562

Cosi fan tutte

104

Così fan tutte   B. & H. 16562

Così fan tutte

Così fan tutte

107

Così fan tutte

B. & H. 16562

Così fan tutte

Così fan tutte

110

Fio.

smart, with dis-dain and fear I.... smart, with dis-dain and fear I smart.
-ror, di di-spet-to e di ter-ror, di di-spet-to e di ter-ror.

Dor.

smart, with dis-dain and fear I.... smart, with dis-dain and fear I smart.
-ror, di di-spet-to e di ter-ror, di di-spet-to e di ter.-ror.

Des.

dart, this de-feat of Cu-pid's dart, this de-feat of Cu-pid's dart.
-ror, quel-la rab-bia e quel fu-ror, quel-la rab-bia e quel fu-ror.

Fer.

dart, this de-feat of Cu-pid's dart, this de-feat of Cu-pid's dart.
-ror, quel-la rab-bia e quel fu-ror, quel-la rab-bia e quel fu-ror.

A.

dart, this de-feat of Cu-pid's dart, this de-feat of Cu-pid's dart.
-ror, quel-la rab-bia e quel fu-ror, quel-la rab-bia e quel fu-ror.

G.

dart, this de-feat of Cu-pid's dart, this de-feat of Cu-pid's dart.
-ror, quel-la rab-bia e quel fu-ror, quel-la rab-bia e quel fu-ror.

RECIT.
Don Alfonso (entering)

What a shin-dy! What hol-ler-ings! What alarms and ex-cursions! What a Ha-des!
Che su-sur-ro! Che stre-pi-to! Che scompi-glio è mai que-sto! Sie-te paz-ze,

A.

Tell me, my dear young ladies, you want the neighbours paying you a vi-sit? What's the matter? What
ca-re le mie ra-gaz-ze? Vo-le-te sol-le-var il vi-ci-na-to? Co-sa a-ve-te? Ch'è

Cosi fan tutte

B. & H. 16562

114

Così fan tutte

B. & H. 16562

sen-ses or our af-fec-tions. No use at all for man to
-rec-chio, e no-stri af-fet-ti! In-van per voi, per gli altri in-

try to tempt us to be false to our faith. The troth we
-van si cer-ca le no-stre al-me se-dur. L'in-tat-ta

plighted, when we first were u-ni-ted here to our
fe-de, che per noi già si die-de ai ca-ria-

lov-ers, we shall know how to keep till death di-vide us,
-man-ti, sa-prem lo-ro ser-bar in-fino a mor-te,

though the world break a-sunder and furies ride us.
a di-spet-to del mondo e del-la sor-te.

№ 14. Aria

Cosi fan tutte

B. & H. 16562

Così fan tutte

122

Così fan tutte

№ 15. Aria

Così fan tutte

SCENE 12

Nº 16. Terzetto

Don Alfonso

Cosi fan tutte

Così fan tutte

B. & H. 16562

Cosi fan tutte

No 17. Aria

Cosi fan tutte

136

Fer.

-ses, pro - vides .... all I need.
-ro al.... cor .... por - ge - rà.

(Exit Ferrando and Guglielmo)

SCENE 13

RECIT.

Don Alfonso

Real-ly, it's quite ri - di - cu - lous! In all this wick-ed world hard-ly a - ny women faithful — and
Oh la sa - ria da ri - de - re: sì po - che son le don - ne co - stanti in questo mondo, e

(Enter Despina)

A.

here we have a pair! They'll ne - ver stand it! Hey, this way, fel - low
qui ve - ne son due! non sa - rà nul - la... Vie - ni, vie - ni, fan-

A.

ban - dit! And come and tell me what goes on here, where you've hid your hand - some
-ciul - la, e dim-mi un po - co do - ve so - no, e che fan le tue pa -

Così fan tutte

138

Così fan tutte

B. & H. 16562

Così fan tutte

Des. When lit-tle me gets pro-per-ly down to busi-ness, she ne-ver makes a
Quan-do De-spi-na mac-chi-na u-na co-sa non può man-car d'ef-

Des. bloom-er. When I re-mem-ber the men I've led in blink-ers, to
-fet-to; ho gia me-na-ti mill' uo-mi-ni pel na-so, sa-

Des. fool these dames is ba-by-work. Come clean, now! Your whis-ker boys are
-prò me-nar due fem-mi-ne. Son ric-chi i due mon-sieurs mu-

Des. weal-thy? And they're now?...
-stac-chi? Do-'ve son?

Don Alfonso
Chock-a-block with it. In the street there, mark-ing
Son rich-is-si-mi. Sul-la stra-da at-ten-

Des. Right, then. Go and fetch 'em. There's a
I - te, e sul fat-to per la

A. time till I call 'em.
- dan - do - mi stan - no.

Des. door you can use that'll take you to the cor - ri - dor and that way you can
pic - cio - la por - ta a me ri - con - du - ce - te - li: v'a - spet - to, nel - la

Des. bring them to my room. If you do what I tell you and fol - low all the
ca - me - ra mi - a. Pur - chè tut - to fac - cia - te quel ch'io v'or - di - ne -

Des. leads, long be-fore morning your mer-ry boys can count u-pon their chickens. Then
- rò pria di do - ma - ni i vo-stri a - mi - ci can-ter-an vit-to - ria; ed

(Exuent)

Des. they will have their din - ners and I my pick - ings.
es - si a - vran-no il gus - to ed io la glo - ria.

SCENE 14. A Garden with lawns on the sides.

Nº 18. Finale

Andante

mezza voce.

Fiordiligi

Ah,............ this day with no to-morrow has un-time-ly marred my for-tune.
Ah .... che tut-ta in un mo-men-to si can-giò la sor-te mi-a,

Dorabella

Ah, this day with no to-morrow has un-time-ly marred my for-tune.
Ah che tut-ta in un mo-men-to si can-giò la sor-te mi-a,

Cosi fan tutte

B. & H. 16564.

144

Cosi fan tutte

B. & H. 16562

Cosi fan tutte

SCENE 15. Ferrando, Guglielmo and Don Alfonso off

Ferrando and Guglielmo enter, each carrying
a phial. Don Alfonso follows.

Cosi fan tutte

Così fan tutte

150

Cosi fan tutte

B. & H. 16562

151

Così fan tutte

B. & H. 16562

152

Cosi fan tutte

B. & H. 16562

Fio. ev - 'ry-one, can't you hear us? Is
gen - te ac-cor-re - te, gen-te! Nes-

Dor. ev - 'ry-one, can't you hear us? Is
gen - te ac-cor-re - te, gen-te! Nes-

Fio. no one, no one near us? De - spi - na! De-spi - na!
-su - no, o Dio, ci sen-te! De-spi - na! De-spi - na!

Dor. no one, no one near us? De - spi - na! De-spi - na!
-su - no, o Dio, ci sen-te! De-spi - na! De-spi - na!

Despina (off)
Someone's
Chi mi

Fio. De - spi - na! De-spi - na!
De - spi - na! De-spi - na!

Dor. De - spi - na! De-spi - na!
De - spi - na! De-spi - na!

Des. (entering)
call-ing? Oh, God save 'em!
chia-ma? Co-sa ve-do!

Des. Cold as the looks you gave 'em, or migh-ty near, I'd say.
Mor-ti i me-schi-ni cre-do, o pros-si-mi a spi - rar.

Don Alfonso
Ah yes, 'tis true, 'tis
Ah, che pur-trop-po è

Cosi fan tutte

B. & H. 16562

Cosi fan tutte

Così fan tutte

Così fan tutte

SCENE 16. Re-enter Don Alfonso with Despina disguised as a doctor.

Ferrando (aside)
De-spi-na play-ing him, see how he's frocked her!
De-spi-na in maschera, che tri-sta pel - le!

Don Alfonso
Ladies, take heart a-gain, here is the doc-tor.
Ec-co-vi il me-di-co, Si-gno-re bel-le!

Guglielmo (aside)
De-spi-na play-ing him, see how he's frocked her!
De-spi-na in maschera, che tri-sta pel - le!

Fiordiligi
What game is this, sir? We cannot play it.
Par-la un linguaggio che non sappia-mo.

Dorabella
What game is this, sir? We cannot play it.
Par-la un linguaggio che non sappia-mo.

Despina
Sal-ve-te a-ma-bi-les bo-nes pu-el-les.
Sal-ve-te a-ma-bi-les bo-nes pu-el-les.
You tell what
Co-me co-

Des.
tongue I say and then I say it. I say Al-ba-ni-an, I say Rou-ma-ni-an, I say in
man-da-no dun-que par-lia-mo, so il gre-co e l'a-ra-bo, so il turco e il van-da-lo, lo sveco e il

Cosi fan tutte

162

Des. A - ra-bic, I say Ba - bu.
tar - ta-ro so an-cor par-lar.

Don Alfonso
I beg you not, sir, be so lin - guis-tic, be so lin-
Tan - ti lin - guag-gi per se con - ser - vi, per se con-

cresc.

A. - guis-tic. See these un - for-tun-ates! Be re - al - is - tic! They've taken
- ser - vi: quei mi - se - ra - bi - li per o - ra os - ser - vi, pre-so han-no il

Fiordiligi
Oh, learned doc - tor, say what's to do.
Si-gnor Dot to - re chè si può far?

Dorabella
Oh, learned doc - tor, say what's to do.
Si-gnor Dot to - re chè si può far?

Despina (examining them)
You'll have to
Sa - per bi-

A. ar - se-nic, so what's to do?
tos - si-co chè si può far?

Des. give me first some in - for-ma-tion a-bout the na-ture of this in-gus-
- so-gna-mi pria la ca-gio - ne e quin-ci l'in-do-le del - la po-

Così fan tutte

B. & H. 16562

164

Così fan tutte

B. & H. 16562

Così fan tutte

B. & H. 16562

Ferrando

Guglielmo

Andante

Do   I
Do   -   ve

Fer. dream?   Or   else where are we?
      son!   *che lo-co è que-sto?*

G.   dream?   Or   else where are we?
      son!   *che lo-co è que-sto?*

Fer. Who are you, sir, and these la-dies?   Have we come where Ju-no's
      Chi è co-lui? co-lor chi so-no?   *Son di Gio-ve in-nan-zi al*

G.   Who are you, sir, and these la-dies?   Have we come where Ju-no's
      Chi è co-lui? co-lor chi so-no?   *Son di Gio-ve in-nan-zi al*

Fer. glade is?   You   are Pal - las?   And you are   Ve-nus?
      tro-no?   *Sei   tu Pal-la,   o Ci-te - re-a?*

G.   glade is?   You   are Pal - las?   And you are   Ve-nus?
      tro-no?   *Sei   tu Pal-la,   o Ci-te - re-a?*

cresc.

Cosi fan tutte   B.& H. 16562

174

Così fan tutte

Così fan tutte

B. & H. 16562

Così fan tutte

182

Così fan tutte

183

Fio. No! You find us here pro-test-ing in the / Ah, che trop-po si ri-chie-de da u-na

Dor. No! You find us here pro-test-ing in the / Ah, che trop-po si ri-chie-de da u-na

Des. don't un-do the work of kind-ness! By your blind-ness, / per ef-fet-to di bon-ta-te, Se-con-da-te, (aside)

Fer. As for / Dal - la (aside)

A. don't un-do the work of kind-ness! By your blind-ness, / per ef-fet-to di bon-ta-te, Se-con-da-te, (aside)

G. As for / Dal - la

Fio. name of faith-ful lov-ers at the fav-our you're re-quest-ing. We are wounded....to the / fi-da o-nes-ta a-man-te ol-trag-gia-ta è la mia fe-de, ol-trag-gia-to è que-sto

Dor. name of faith-ful lov-ers at the fav-our you're re-quest-ing. We are wounded....to the / fi-da o-nes-ta a-man-te ol-trag-gia-ta è la mia fe-de, ol-trag-gia-to è que-sto

Des. by your blind-ness, by your blindness don't un-do the work of / se - con-da - te, se - con-da - te per ef-fet - to di bon-

Fer. laugh - ter, I shall die of it: it ex-udes from ev'-ry / vo - glia Ch'ho di ri-de-re il pol-mon mi scoppia or-

A. by your blind - ness don't un-do the work of / se - con-da - te per ef-fet - to di bon -

G. laugh - ter, I shall die of it: it ex-udes from ev'-ry / vo - glia Ch'ho di ri-de-re il pol-mon mi scoppia or-

Così fan tutte

Cosi fan tutte

186

Così fan tutte

B. & H. 16562

Cosi fan tutte

188

Così fan tutte

B. & H. 16562

Cosi fan tutte

Così fan tutte

Così fan tutte

Così fan tutte

Così fan tutte
B. & H. 16562
End of Act I

ACT II

198

Des. fly-ing. What a-bout it? Your pair of gallant captains are a-way in the arm-y. For the du-
stes-so, per e-sem-pio: i vo-stri Ga-ni-me-di son an - da - ti al-la guer-ra; in fin che

Dorabella

May hea-ven's angels guard us!
Il cie-lo ce ne guar-di.

Des. -ra-tion, then, fol-low the army fashion— go re-cruiting!
tor-na-no fa-te al-la mi-li-ta-re: re-clu-ta-te.

Oh!
Eh!

Des. But you aren't in heav'n and I'm no angel. Still, trust in my de-vo-tion. You observed your friends' e-
che noi sia-mo in ter-ra, e non in cie-lo! Fi-da-te-vi al mio ze-lo. Giac-chè que-sti fo-re-

Des. -mo-tion— they wor-ship you, so let yourselves be loved. They're wealthy, hand-some,
-stie-ri v'a-do-ra-no, la-scia-te-vi a-do-rar. Son ric-chi, bel-li,

Des. gen-tle-men, o-pen-hand-ed, as your old friend Don Al-fon-so has
no-bi-li, ge-ne-ro-si, co-me fe-de fe-ce a voi Don Al-

Così fan tutte

B. & H. 16562

Des. told you: they had the guts to welcome death just for you. Qualities, sure-ly, that are not to be
-fon-so; a-ve-an cor-rag-gio di mo - ri - re per voi; que-sti son mer-ti che sprezzar non si

Des. sneezed at by ladies such as you, figures of beauty, who owe love, but not lo-vers, proper
den - no da gio-va - ni qual voi bel-le e ga-lan-ti, che pon star sen-za amor, non sen-za a-

Fiordiligi
You're leading us in earnest in-to a low temp-
Per Bac-co ci fa - re-sti far del-le bel-le

Des. (aside)
du - ty. (Gol-ly, I think they're rising.)
-man-ti. (Par che ci tro - vin gu-sto.)

Fio. -ta-tion. Do you think we'd de - mean us just to be-come the toys of a minute, when
co - se; cre-di tu che vo - glia-mo fa-vo-la di-ven-tar de-gli o-zio-si? Ai

Fio. if we but be-gin it we shall strike to the heart those who a-dore us?
no-stri ca - ri spo-si cre-di tu che vo-gliam dar tal tor-men-to.

Despina
But who says that would
E chi di - ce, che ab-

Così fan tutte   B. & H. 16562

Dorabella

Don't you think, though, if they once got to hear it, they
Non ti pa - re, che sia tor - to ba-stan - te, se

Des.

happen, if you did take the others?
- bia - te a far lo - ro al-cun tor - to?

Dor.

might get the im - press - ion we were not be - ing true?
no - to si fa - ces - se che trat - tia - mo co - stor?

Des.

Ea - sy as
An che per

Des.

wink - ing! We'll see they ne - ver hear of it. I'll put a - bout the
que - sto c'è un mez - zo si - cu - ris - si - mo. Io vo - glio spar - ger

Dorabella

But who'd believe you?
Chi vuoi che il cre - da?

Des.

sto - ry your friends are af - ter me. Oh, Christmas! That's a good one!
fa - ma, che ven - go - no da me. Oh bel - la! non ha for - se

Don't you be-lieve a ser-vant de-serves a pair of lo-vers? You can be
mer-to u-na ca-me-rie-ra d'a-ver due ci-cis-be-i? Di me fi-

Fiordiligi

No, no! My heart dis-mis-ses the appeal of your strangers. They e-ven were so
No, no, son trop-po au-da-ci que-sti tuoi fo-re-stie-ri, non eb-ber la bal-

con-fi-dent!
- da - te - vi.

forward as to pray for our kiss-es.
- dan-za fin di chie-der dei ba - ci.

(Oo, how awful!) I tru-ly can as-sure you that their
(Che dis-gra-zia!) io pos-so as-si-cu-rar-vi, che le

ug - ly be-ha-viour was en-tire-ly the fault of all that
co - se che han fat-to, fu-ro ef-fet-to del tos-si-co, che han

poi - son; their con-vul-sions, their rav-ings, their queer-ness, their fun-ny
pre - so, con-vul-sio-ni, de-li-ri, fol-li-e, va-neg-gia-

Così fan tutte

B. & H. 16562

202

Cosi fan tutte

B. & H. 16562

Des.

While men are jo - king, she'll be pro - vo - king, see without star - ing, guess what's pre-
Dee in un mo - men - to dar ret-ta a cen - to, col-le pu - pil - le par-lar con

- par - ing.
mil - le.
Hand - some and ug - ly, she'll treat 'em
Dar spe - me a tut - ti, sien bel-li o

snug - ly, making her get - a-way look like the bet-ter way, swim without sinking, fib with-out
brut - ti, sa - per na-scon-der-si, sen-za con-fon-der-si, sen-za ar-ros - si-re sa-per men-

blink-ing, fib with-out blink-ing. Once they have seen it, men know you mean it, then you can
- ti - re, sa-per men - ti - re. E qual re - gi - na dall' al - to so - glio col pos-so e

f p   *f p*   *f p*

queen it, treating 'em rough.
vo - glio far-si ub-bi - dir,
Once they have seen it, then you can
e qual re - gi - na col pos-so e

f p   *f p*   *f p*

Cosi fan tutte

B. & H. 16562

(to herself)

Des. queen it, treating 'em rough. I think they like it—
vo - glio far-si ub-bi - dir. *Par ch'ab-bian gu-sto*

Des. soon they'll come cleaner. God bless De- spi-na, she knows her stuff, she knows her stuff.
di tal dot-tri - na, vi - va De- spi-na, che sa ser - vir,.....che sa ser-vir.

Des. While men are jo - king, she'll be pro - vok-ing, see without
Dee in un mo - men - to dar ret-ta a cen - to, col - le pu -

Des. star-ing, guess what's pre-par-ing. Hand-some and
-pil - le par-lar con mil - le. *Dar spe-me a*

Des. ug - ly, she'll treat 'em snug-ly, mak-ing her get - away look like the bet-ter way, swim without
tut - ti, sien bel - li o brut - ti, sa - per na-scon-der-si, sen - za con-fon-der-si, sen - za ar-ros-

Così fan tutte

SCENE 2
RECIT.

Cosi fan tutte

B. & H. 16562

Così fan tutte

Così fan tutte

Cosi fan tutte

216

Fio.
light and en-joy-ing gay de-light,..... and en-joy-ing gay de-light.
-rò, che spasset-to io pro-ve-rò,......... che spas-set-to io pro-ve-rò!

Dor.
light and en-joy-ing gay de-light,..... and en-joy-ing gay de-light.
-rò, che spasset-to io pro-ve-rò,......... che spas-set-to io pro-ve-rò!

cresc.

f

tr

SCENE 3
RECIT.
Don Alfonso
Come, make haste to the gar-den, my en-chant-ing young ladies. Too de-licious! Such
Ah, cor-re-te al giar-di-no! Le mie ca-re ra-gaz-ze! Che al-le-gria! che

A.
junketings! Such singing! What a pa-geant of har-mony! What magic! Hurry up, now, we're
mu-si-ca! Che can-to! Che bril-lan-te spet-ta-co-lo! Che in-canto! Fa-te pre-sto, cor-

Dorabella
What e-ver is a-foot?
Che dia-mi-ne es-ser può?

A.
go-ing. You'll soon be know-ing.
-re-te! To-sto ve-dre-te.

Così fan tutte

B. & H. 16562

SCENE 4. A garden by the sea, with seats and stone tables. At the landing place a barge decorated with flowers. In the barge are Ferrando and Guglielmo with singers and musicians. Despina is in the garden. Fiordiligi and Dorabella, led by Don Alfonso, enter at one side.

Nº 21. Duet and Chorus

218

Così fan tutte

B. & H. 16562

220

Così fan tutte

B. & H. 16562

№ 22. Quartet

Don Alfonso (Taking Dorabella by the hand)

B. & H.

Allegretto grazioso

p

Come, give me your fin-ger and stir yourself,
La ma-no a me da - te, mo - ve - te - vi un

do.
pò!

(To the lovers)

If your answers lin-ger, I'll make 'em for
Se voi non par - la - te, per voi par - le -

you, I'll make 'em for you, I'll make 'em for you.
- rò, per voi par - le - rò, per voi par - le - rò.

May
Per-

grace be ex- tend-ed to this your poor ser-vant:
- do - no vi chie-de un schia-vo tre-man-te!

He
V'of-

knows he's of-fend-ed by be-ing too fervent.
-fe - se, lo ve-de, ma so-lo un i-stan-te;

He's si-lent from an-guish,
Or pe - na, ma ta - ce,

Così fan tutte

Exit Despina and Don Alfonso

Così fan tutte

SCENE 5

232

Così fan tutte

B. & H. 16562

Così fan tutte

№ 23. Duet

B. & H. 16562

Così fan tutte

Fer.

like - ly, till one glance from your eyes my heart has mend - ed? Oh,
-rar - lo, se pria gli oc - chi men fie - ri a me non gi - ri. O

Fer.

heav'n! If she will grant it, my sigh - ing's end - ed.
ciel! Ma tu mi guar - di, e poi so - spi - ri?

№ 24. Aria

(Very gaily)

Ferrando

Allegretto

Ne - ver tell me this ex - qui - site beauty will desire my de - vo - tion a - way Or de -
Ah! Io veg - gio: quell'a - ni - ma bel - la al mio pian - to re - si - ster non sà, non è

Fer.

- ny the re - ward of a du - ty .... I de - light with af - fec - tion to pay,..... or de -
fat - ta per es - ser ru - bel - la .... a - gli af - fet - ti di a - mi - ca pie - tà,....... Non è

Fer.

- ny the re - ward of a du - ty, a du - ty, I de - light .... with af - fect - ion to
fat - ta per es - ser ru - bel - la, ru - bel - la agli af - fet - ti di a - mi - ca pie -

Cosi fan tutte   B. & H. 16562

242

Cosi fan tutte

B. & H. 16562

244

248

Cosi fan tutte

B. & H. 16562

No 25. Rondo

Così fan tutte

SCENE 8
RECIT.
(In high spirits)

Ferrando: My dear boy! We're on a win-ner! I can report on
A - mi - co, ab - bia - mo vin - to! U - na cinquinta, a -

Guglielmo: We both are? Or I am?
Un am - bo, o un ter - no?

Fer.: your nag. Fior-di-li-gi— all that a nice girl should be. No sign of it. Just
- mi - co; Fior-di-li-gi— è la mo-de-stia in car-ne. Nien-tis-si-mo; sta at-

G.: Nothing less, then?
Nien-te me - no?

Fer.: lis-ten, I'll tell you how it went. You saw us strolling
- ten-to, e a-scol-ta co - me fù. Pel giar-di-net - to,

G.: I'll hear you quite con-tent.
T'a-scol-to; di pur sù.

Fer.: down by the lit-tle ter-race? Well, there I start ca-jol-ing; take her el-bow, we chatter, we
co-me e-ra-vam d'accor-do, a pas-seg-giar mi met-to; le do il brac-cio; si par-la di

Cosi fan tutte

B. & H. 16562

Cosi fan tutte

№ 26. Aria

Allegretto

Guglielmo

Girls, you
Don - ne

G.

know you're al-ways at it, at it, at it, at it, at........it!
mie, la fa - te a tan-ti,a tan-ti, a tan-ti,a tan-ti,a tan - ti!

G.

Since in truth I take a pride, when the men complain you've rat-ted I am
Che se il ver vi deg-gio dir, se si la-gna-no gli a - man-ti, li co-

G.

ra-ther on their side, I am ra-ther on their side.
- min-cio a com-pa - tir, li co - min-cio a com-pa - tir.

B. & H. 16562

266

and you of - ten make me sick.
m'av - vi - li - sce in ve - ri - tà,

Yes, you of - ten make me
m'av - vi - li - sce in ve - ri -

sick.
- tà.

Your in - ten - tion's al - ways splen - did:
Mil - le vol - te il bran - do pre - si.

I've had ar - gu - ments ga - lore. Your in - ten - tions,
per sal - var il vo-stro o-nor. Mil - le vol - te,

your in-
mil - le

- ten - tions,
vol - te,

your in - ten - tions I've de - fend - ed till my heart and tongue are
mil - le vol - te vi di - fe - si col - la boc - ca e più col

sore.
cor.

But
Ma

you girls are al - ways, al - ways, al - ways at it:
quel far-la a tan-ti e tan-ti, a tan-ti e tan-ti

Cosi fan tutte

268

G. at it: for I can-not tell a lie, no, I cannot tell a
tan-ti, che cre-di-bi-le non è, che cre-di-bi-le non

G. lie. I have found the sex con-genial, mere-ly venial, your in-tentions al-ways
è. Io vo' be-ne al ses-so vo-stro, ve lo mostro, mil-le vol-te il bran-do

fp

G. splendid I've de-fend-ed, ev-'ry grace to tease the eye, When you
pre-si, vi di-fe-si, gran te-so-ri il ciel vi diè, si-no ai

G. try; Girls! Girls! Girls! Why are you al-ways at it, yes,
piè; ma, ma, ma la fa-te a tan-ti e tan-ti, a

G. always, always at it, yes, always at it, at it, at it, at it?
tan-ti e tan-ti, a tan-ti, la fa-te a tan-ti e tan-ti, a tan-ti e tan-ti.

G.

why, the rea - son why, do we know the rea - son why?
chè, un gran per - chè, han - no cer - to un gran per - chè.

(Exit)

SCENE 9

Ferrando

Here am I in con - fusion, with my ideas and my deepest
In qual fie - ro con - tra - sto, in qual disor - di - ne di pen -

Allegro

Fer.

feel - ings a prey to sheer de - so - la - tion.
sie - ri e di af - fet - ti io mi ri - tro - vo.

My unique sit - u -
Tan - to in - so - li - to e

Fer.

- a - tion is such a low one — I must face it — there's no one fit - ted to give me counsel.
no - vo è il ca - so mi - o, che non al - tri, non i - o... ba - sto per con - si - gliar - mi...

Cosí fan tutte

№ 27. Cavatina

Cosi fan tutte

B. & H. 16562

Don Alfonso

could she take an-o-ther? A cas-ual est-i-mate— I hate to blow my
-car pos-sa a un Gu-gliel-mo? Un pic-ciol cal-co-lo, non par-lo per lo-

trum-pet— you must real-ly ad-mit— I loathe to hurt you— there's
-dar-mi, se fac-cia-mo tra noi... Tu ve-di, a-mi-co, che un

Re-ward of vir-tue!
Eh! anch'io lo di-co!

just that lit-tle some-thing. I think you'd bet-ter
po-co di può mer-to. In-tan-to mi da-

I'll be glad to. But be-fore I shell out—one more ad-
Vo-lon-tie-ri: pria pe-rò di pa-gar, vo che fac-

pay me that lit-tle sum you owe me.
-re-te cin-quan-ta zec-chi-net-ti.

B. & H. 16562

Così fan tutte

SCENE 10. A room with several doors, tables and a mirror.

RECIT.

Dorabella

Despina: 'Pon my word, you've come on, miss. Quite a lady of fash-ion.
O - ra ve - do che sie - te u - na don - na di gar - bo.

Dor.: use-less to at-tempt to re-sist. That lit-tle de-vil has such a
-spi - na, di re - si - ster ten - tai: quel de - mo - niet - to ha un ar - ti-

Dor.: me-thod, a way of talk-ing, a man-ner, you'd come down with a crash if you were
-fi - zio, un e - lo-quen - za, un trat - to, che ti fà ca - der giù se sei di

Dor.: granite.
sas - so.

Despina: A-dam and Eve be-gan it! That means to say 'good sense'. S'ever so seldom us
Cor-po di Sa - ta-nas - so! Que - sto vuol dir sa - per! Tan - to di ra - ro noi

Des.: girls can see con-ven-ient to do our-selves a fav-our. When you
po - ve - re ra - gaz - ze ab - bia-mo un po' di be - ne, che bi-

Cosi fan tutte

B. & H. 16562

(enter Fiordiligi)

Des. do pick a plum, en-joy the fla-vour! Look out, now! Here's your sis-ter! Such
-so-gna pi-gliar-lo all-or ch'ei vie-ne. Ma ec-co la so-rel-la, che

Fiordiligi

Oh, you ras-cal! See what a pass I've come to! And it's
Scia-gu-ra-te! Ec-co per col-pa vo-stra in che

Des. dol-drums!
cef-fo!

Fio. your fault en-tire-ly.
sta-to mi tro-vo!

Dorabella

You've such a queer de-
Hai qual-che mal, so-

Des. What's the matter? Come, tell your old De-spi-na.
Co-sa è na-to, ca-ra Ma-da-mi-gel-la?

Fio. A plague on all our hous-es— yours, mine, her's too: Don Al-fon-so's,
Ho il dia-vo-lo, che por-ti me, te, le-i, Don Al-fon-so,

Dor. -mean-our.
-rel-la?

Così fan tutte

Fio. his pair of jack-als and on this whole world of zan-ies!
i fo-re-stie-ri e quan-ti paz - zi ha il mon-do.

Dor. Are you out of your
Hai per-du-to il giu-

Fio. Worse, oh, much worse! Now I shall shock you. I love him! And "him" in this case is-n't
Peg-gio, peg-gio, in - or-ri-dis-ci: io a-mo! e l'a-mor mi-o non è

Dor. sen-ses?
- di-zio?

Fio. quite my Gugliel-mo.
sol per Gu-gliel-mo.

Dor. And are you tell-ing me that you have fal - len
E che si, che an-che tu se' in-na-mo-ra - ta

Despina
Goo-dy, goo-dy!
Me-glio, me-glio!

(sighing)

Fio. Ah! Too much for my peace!
Ah, pur trop - po per noi.

Dor. for the good - look-ing fair one?
del ga - lan - te bion-di - no?

Des. Oh, splen-did!
Ma bra - va!

Cosi fan tutte

282

№ 28. Aria

Dor. straight your soul he cag - es and li - ber - ty de - nies. .... Ah, Love's a gay de-
l'a - ni - ma in ca - te - na, e to - glie li - ber - tà. .... È a - mo - re un la - dron-

cresc. *f* *p*

Dor. - cei - ver, a make be - lieve is he; .... he sends you sad or joy - ful, or
- cel - lo, un ser - pen - tel - lo a - mor, ... ei to - glie e dà .... la pa - ce, la

Dor. joy - ful, af - ter his coy ... de - cree. Mirth and con - tent - ing, con-
pa - ce, co - me gli pia - ce ai cor. Por - ta dol - cez - za, dol-

Dor. - tent .... and fav - ours he'll bring, if you'll o - bey. ..... But if your du - ty
- cez - za e gu - sto, se tu lo la - sci far, ... Ma t'em - pie di dis-

fp

Dor. wa - vers, but if your du - ty wa - vers, he takes them all a - way.
- gu - sto, ma t'em - pie di dis - gu - sto, se ten - ti di pu - gnar.

fp *fp* *fp* *f* *p*

Così fan tutte

B. & H. 16562

Così fan tutte

Cosi fan tutte

288

Dor.

fear, no fear, like me, and have no fear.
-sì, co-sì, che anch' io fa-rò co-sì!

f

(Exit Dorabella and Despina)

SCENE 11. Fiordiligi alone; later Guglielmo, Ferrando and Don Alfonso. They are seen through an open door in an adjoining room.

RECIT.

Fiordiligi

All the world is conspir-ing to be-tray my poor heart. But no! I'll per-ish before I
Co-me tut-to con-giu-ra a se-dur-re il mio cor! Ma no! Si mo-ra, e non si

Fio.

yield it. 'Twas wrong to tell my sis-ter and my ser-vant the weak-ness I was feel-ing.
ce-da! Er-rai, quando al-la suo-ra io mi sco-per-si ed al-la ser-va mi-a.

Fio.

Now they'll tell him the sto-ry to make him stron-ger— I can stand it no
Es-se a lui di-ran tut-to, ed ei più au-da-ce, fia di tut-to ca-

Così fan tutte   B. & H. 16562

Fio.

act - ing with-out my know - ledge... Soft - ly! I've re-mem-bered there's a
sen - za sa - pu - ta mi - a... *Pia - no!* *Un pen - sie - ro per la*

way I can stop it. Up in our clo - sets are u - ni-forms in plen - ty
men - te mi pas - sa; in ca - sa mi - a re - star mol-te u - ni - for - mi

of Gu-gliel - mo's and Fer - ran - do's. Now quick! De - spi - na! De-
di Gu-gliel - mo e di Fer - ran - do, ar - dir! De - spi - na! De-

- spi - na! Take this key and be off now— and no back answer - ing,
- spi - na! Tie - ni un po' que-sta chia - ve e sen - za re - pli - ca,

Despina (enters)

Here I am.
Co - sa c'è!

no back answers what-ev - er— go to the wal - nut ward-robe and bring me
sen - za re - pli - ca al-cu - na, pren - di nel guar-da - ro - ba, e qui mi

292

Cosi fan tutte

B. & H. 16562

SCENE 12. Fiordiligi, later Ferrando; Guglielmo and Don Alfonso are seen in the other room.

Così fan tutte

№ 29. Duet

Fio.
me! Un-lucky chan-ces come to tor-ture my ex-istence.
-mè! Son ab-ba-stan-za tor-men-ta-ta, ed in-fe-li-ce!
Fer.
Ah,..... my plead-ing, my fond
Ah,.....che o-mai la.... sua co-
Fio.
Ah,...... his pleading, his fond glances, now.... af-
Ah,.....che o-mai la... mia co-stan-za, a .... quei
Fer.
glances, now.... af-fect her brave re-sistance,
stan-za, a.........quei sguar-di, a quel che di-ce,
Fio.
-fect my brave re-sistance, Make me wa-ver af-ter all,...make me wa-ver af-ter
sguardi, a quel che di-ce, in-co-min-cia a va-cil-lar, in-co-min-cia a va-cil-
Fer.
Make her wa-ver af-ter all, make her wa-ver af-ter
In-co-min-cia a va-cil-lar, in-co-min-cia a va-cil-
cresc.
p
Fio.
all,... make me wa-ver af-ter all. Rise now, rise....... now!
-lar,.... in-co-min-cia a va-cil-lar. Sor-gi, sor-gi.
Fer.
all, make her wa-ver af-ter all. In.... vain you
-lar, in-co-min-cia a va-cil-lar. In-van lo
cresc.
p

Così fan tutte

Così fan tutte

Così fan tutte

SCENE 13

RECIT.

Guglielmo

Oh, what a dread-ful thing! To think I saw it! And that I ev-en
Oh po-ve-ret-to me, Co-sa ho ve-du-to! Co-sa ho sen-ti-to

Don Alfonso

For God's sake keep your mouth shut!
Per ca-ri-tà! si-len-zio!

heard it!
ma-i!

I'll tear my hair in hand-fuls! I'll
Mi pe-le-rei la bar-ba! Mi

slit my wretched gul-let! Then the horns on my head can scare the mul-let. Was that my Fior-di-
graf-fie-rei la pel-le! E da-rei col-le cor-na en-tro le stel-le, fu quel-la Fior-di-

-li-gi? The Pe-ne-lo-pe, the Di-a-na of now-a-days! De-ceiv-er! Common baggage! De-
-li-gi! La Pe-ne-lo-pe, l'Ar-te-mi-sia del se-co-lo? Bric-co-na, as-sas-si-na fur-

B. & H. 16562

304

A. wo-men made of su-gar just to suit your com-plex-ions. In such-like
don-ne d'al-tra pa-sta, per i vo-stri bei mu-si; in o-gni

A. mat-ters you must be phi-lo-soph-ic. So come a-long, then: by
co-sa ci vuol fi-lo-so-fi-a. Ve-ni-te me-co: di

A. pro-cess of de-duct-ion we shall reach a so-lu-tion. And the
com-bi-nar le co-se stu-die-rem la ma-nie-ra. Vo che an-

A. first con-tri-bu-tion is to wed them as spec-i-fied. But
-cor que-sta se-ra dop-pie noz-ze si fac-cia-no: frat-

A. first,though, let me sing you a sonnet, full of splendid ad-vice. Re-flect up-on it.
-tan-to un' ot-ta-va as-col-ta-te: fe-li-cis-si-mi voi se la im-pa-ra-te.

Così fan tutte   B. & H. 16562

SCENE 14

RECIT.

Despina

Hur-rah, you've pulled 'em ov-er. Made their minds up to
Vit - to - ria pa - dron - ci - ni! A spo-sar - vi dis-

wed you, have your sweet pair of la-dies. I took a chance and prom-ised 'em in
-spo - ste son le ca - re ma - da - me: a no-me vo-stro lo - ro io pro-

your names you would take 'em with you in say three days at la-test. Now I've my
- mi - si, che in tre gior - ni cir - ca par-ti - ran - no con vo - i. L'or-din mi

or-ders to pro-cure 'em a law-yer to draft the mar-riage
die - ro di tro-var un no - ta - jo, che sti - pu-li il con-

con-tracts. Up in their draw-ing-room they a - wait your ar - ri - val.
- trat - to: al - la lor ca - me - ra at - ten - den - do - vi stan - no.

Nº 31. Finale

SCENE 15. A Saloon, with an orchestra in the background. A table laid for four persons. Despina, servants and musicians; later Don Alfonso.

Allegro assai

Così fan tutte

Despina

Quick-ly, all, a-bout your business! Let the torches now be light - ed _ And the
Fa - te pres-to, o ca-ri a - mi - ci, al - le fa-ci il fo - co da - te, è la

Des. ta - bles rich - ly dight - ed, as be - fits no - bi - li -
men - sa pre - pa - ra - te, con ric - chez - za e no - bil -

Des. - ty. For the mar - riage of the la - dies is the
- tà. Del - le no - stre pa - dron - ci - ne gl'i - me -

Des. cause for ce - le - bra - tion. Hur - ry now.... and.... take your
- nei son già dis - po - sti, e voi gi - te ai vo - stri

Des. sta - tion, ere the hap - py pairs you see, ere the hap - py pairs you
po - sti... fin - chè i spo - si.... ven - gon quà, fin - chè i spo - si ven - gon

Cosi fan tutte

SCENE 16

Così fan tutte

B. & H. 16562

318

B. & H. 16562

319

Così fan tutte

B. & H. 16562

Così fan tutte

Cosi fan tutte

Cosi fan tutte

B. & H. 16562

Cosi fan tutte

B. & H. 16562

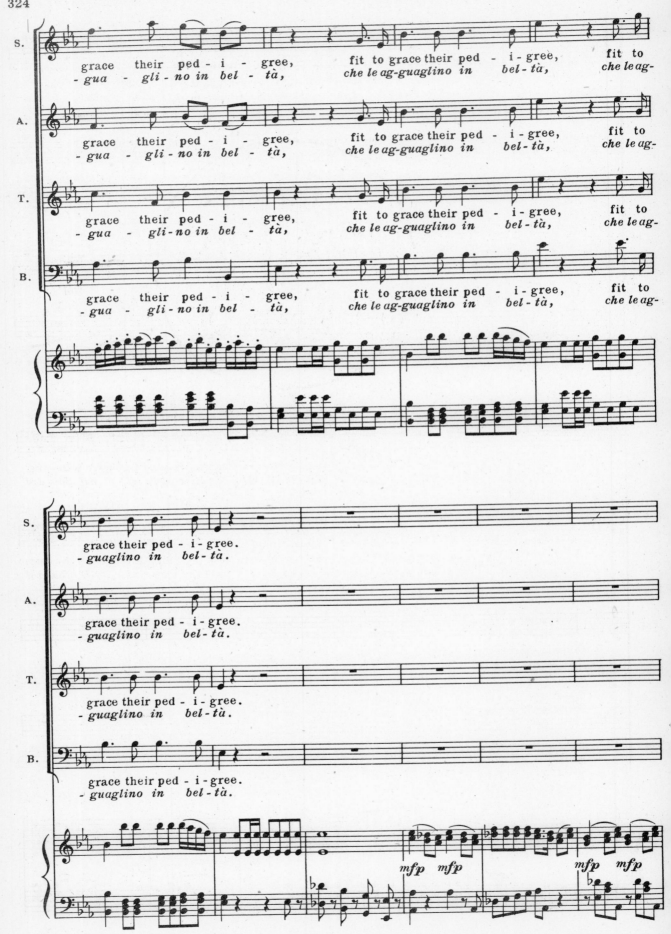

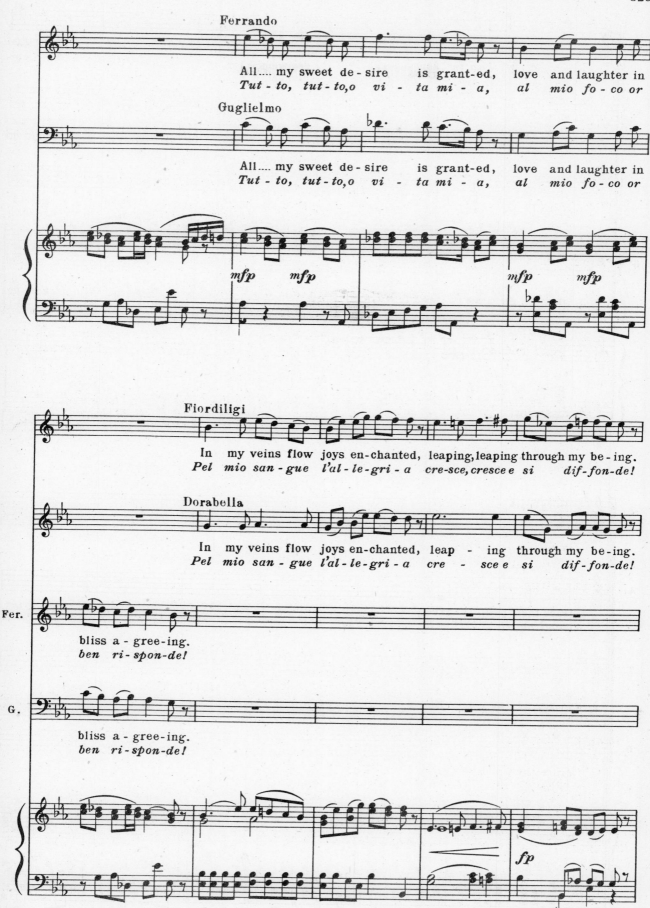

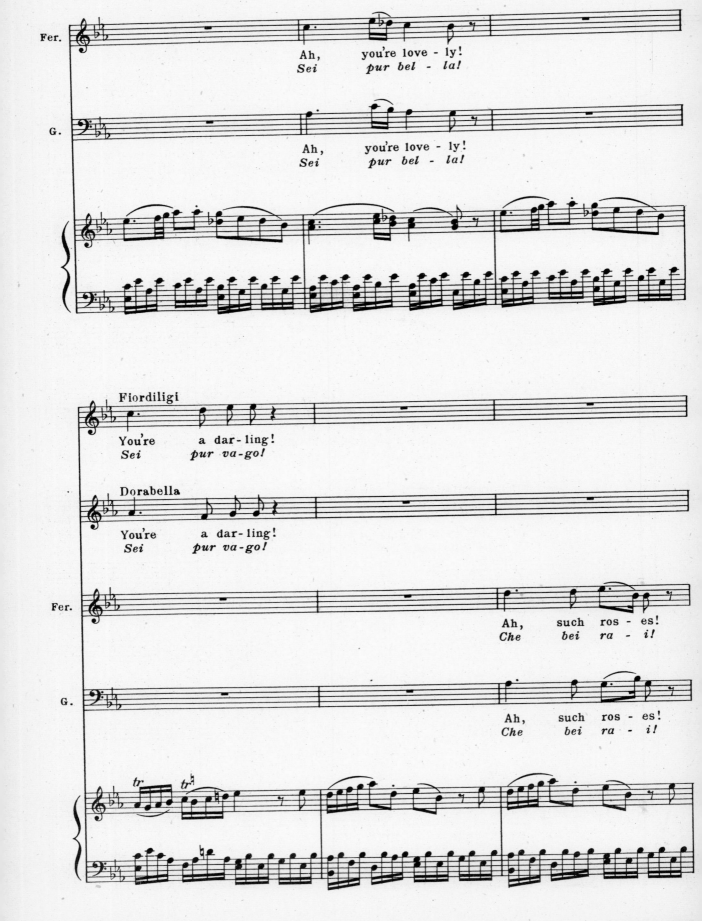

B. & H. 16562

Cosí fan tutte

SCENE 17

Don Alfonso

Allegro

Fiordiligi

Splendid, splendid! Can't you hur-ry him?
Bra-vo, bra-vo! Pas-si su-bi-to.

Dorabella

Splendid, splendid! Can't you hur-ry him?
Bra-vo, bra-vo! Pas-si su-bi-to.

Ferrando

Splendid, splendid! Can't you hur-ry him?
Bra-vo, bra-vo! Pas-si su-bi-to.

A.

stair-case; ip-so fac-to he'll ap-pear.   Let me
sca-le, e ip-so fac-to qui ver-rà.   *Vò a chia-*

Guglielmo

Splendid, splendid! Can't you hur-ry him?
Bra-vo, bra-vo! Pas-si su-bi-to.

A.

call him, let me call him.   Now he is here.
mar-lo, vò a chia-mar-lo;   *ec-co-lo quà!*

(Enter Despina)

Despina

Bear-ing hope of fu-ture bless-ing, I'm the lawyer Bec-ca-vi-vi, as is
Au-gu-ran-do-vi o-gni be-ne, il no-ta-jo Bec-ca-vi-vi coll' u-

Des.

meet, cor-rect-ly dress-ing in my ce-re-mon-ial gear.
-sa-ta a voi sen vie-ne no-ta-ria-le di-gni-tà!

Cosi fan tutte

B. & H. 16562

332

Così fan tutte

B. & H. 16562

B. & H. 16562

Cosi fan tutte

336

Cosi fan tutte

B. & H. 16562

Cosi fan tutte

Così fan tutte

340

Cosi fan tutte

B. & H. 16562

Così fan tutte

Così fan tutte

Così fan tutte

Così fan tutte

Così fan tutte

Così fan tutte

Così fan tutte

Fiordiligi *(sotto voce)*

Bless-ed.... he who meets with patience ev - 'ry chance in high good hum-our
For - tu - na - to l'uom che pren-de o - gni co-sa pel buon ver-so,

Dorabella *(sotto voce)*

Bless-ed.... he who meets with patience ev - 'ry chance in high good hum-our
For - tu - na - to l'uom che pren-de o - gni co - sa pel buon ver-so,

Despina *(sotto voce)*

Bless-ed he who meets with patience ev - 'ry chance in high good hum-our
For - tu - na - to l'uom che pren-de o - gni co - sa pel buon ver-so,

Ferrando *(sotto voce)*

Bless-ed.... he who meets with pat-ience ev - 'ry chance in high good hum-our
For - tu - na - to l'uom che pren-de o - gni co - sa pel buon ver-so,

Don Alfonso *(sotto voce)*

Bless-ed he who meets with patience ev - 'ry chance in high good hum-our
For - tu - na - to l'uom che pren-de o - gni co - sa pel buon ver-so,

Guglielmo *(sotto voce)*

Bless-ed he who meets with patience ev - 'ry chance in high good hum-our
For - tu - na - to l'uom che pren-de o - gni co - sa pel buon ver-so,

Fio.

and in tri-als and tri-bu - lations lets his rea - son..... show the
e tra i ca-si, e le vi-cen-de da ra - gion gui - dar si

Dor.

and in tri-als and tri-bu - lations lets his rea - son..... show the
e tra i ca-si, e le vi-cen-de da ra - gion gui - dar si

Des.

and in tri-als and tri-bu - lations lets his rea - son..... show the
e tra i ca-si, e le vi-cen-de da ra - gion gui - dar si

Fer.

and in tri-als and tri-bu - lations lets his rea - son..... show the
e tra i ca-si, e le vi-cen-de da ra - gion gui - dar si

A.

and in tri-als and tri-bu - lations lets his rea - son show the
e tra i ca-si, e le vi-cen-de da ra - gion gui - dar si

G.

and in tri-als and tri-bu - lations lets his rea - son show the
e tra i ca-si, e le vi-cen-de da ra - gion gui - dar si

Così fan tutte

B. & H. 16562

Così fan tutte

B. & H. 16562

Così fan tutte

B. & H. 16562

THE ROYAL EDITION
OF SONG BOOKS AND OPERATIC ALBUMS

SONGS OF ENGLAND. *Three Volumes. Edited by J. L. Hatton and Eaton Faning.*

SONGS OF SCOTLAND. *Two Volumes. Edited by Colin Brown, J. Pittman, Myles B. Foster, Dr. C. Mackay.*

SONGS OF IRELAND. *Edited by J. L. Hatton and J. L. Molloy.*

SONGS OF WALES. *Edited by Brinley Richards.*

MANX NATIONAL SONGS. *Edited by Dr. J. Clague and W. H. Gill.*

SONGS OF FRANCE. *With French and English words.*

SONGS OF ITALY. *With Italian and English words.*

SONGS OF SCANDINAVIA. *Edited by J. A. Kappey.*

SONGS OF GERMANY. *With German and English words.*

BEETHOVEN'S SONGS. *With German and English words.*

HANDEL'S OPERA SONGS. *Edited by W. T. Best.*

MENDELSSOHN'S SONGS AND DUETS. *Edited by J. Pittman.*

MOZART'S SONGS. *With German, Italian and English words.*

RUBINSTEIN'S SONGS. *New Edition.*

RUBINSTEIN'S DUETS. *Edited by H. Eisoldt.*

SCHUBERT'S SONGS. *Two Volumes, edited by J. A. Kappey.*

SCHUMANN'S SONGS. *Edited by J. L. Hatton.*

SONGS OF THE ORATORIOS. *Edited by M. B. Foster.*

SONGS FROM THE OPERAS. *Two Volumes.*

MODERN BALLADS *by Sullivan, Molloy, Gatty, Marzials, etc.*

HUMOROUS SONGS. *Edited by J. L. Hatton.*

DUETS FOR LADIES' VOICES. *Edited by Randagger.*

THE PRIMA DONNA'S ALBUM. *46 Songs for Soprano.*

THE CONTRALTO ALBUM. *50 Songs.*

THE TENOR ALBUM. *52 Songs.*

THE BARITONE ALBUM. *45 Songs.*

BOOSEY & HAWKES, LTD.

London · Paris · Bonn · Capetown · Sydney · Toronto · New York

No. 427

HENRY PURCELL

Realisations by BENJAMIN BRITTEN

ORPHEUS BRITANNICUS

Seven Songs, *for High or Medium Voice and Piano*

Fairest Isle. If music be the food of love (*3rd version*). Turn then thine eyes. Music for a while. Pious Celinda. I'll sail upon the Dog-Star. On the brow of Richmond Hill.

Six Songs, *for High or Medium Voice and Piano*

Mad Bess. If music be the food of love (*1st version*). Man is for the woman made (*also published separately*). There is not a swain in the plain. Not all my torments. Sweeter than roses.

Suite of Songs, *for High Voice and Small Orchestra*

Let sullen discord smile. Why should men quarrel? So when the glittering Queen of Night. Thou tunest this world. 'Tis holiday. Sound fame thy Brazen Trumpet.

ODES AND ELEGIES

The Queen's Epicedium, *for High Voice and Piano*

HARMONIA SACRA

The Blessed Virgin's Expostulation, *for High Voice and Piano*
Job's Curse, *for High Voice and Piano*
Saul and the Witch at Endor, *for Soprano, Tenor, Bass and Piano*
Three Divine Hymns, *for High or Medium Voice and Piano*
We sing to Him. Evening Hymn. Lord, what is man?

G. F. HANDEL

A Collection of Songs selected and edited by Walter Ford
Piano accompaniments newly arranged by Rupert Erlebach

VOLUME I : LIGHT SOPRANO

Guardian Angel (*Time and Truth*). Sinners, lift your eyes (*Second Passion*). O killing shock (*Athalia*). Author of peace (*Saul*). Straight mine eye has caught new pleasure (*L'Allegro*). Me, when the sun begins to shine (*Il Pensieroso*). No, no, I'll take no less (*Seville*). O lovely youth (*Joseph*). As cheers the sun (*Joshua*). No more shall armed bands (*Solomon*).

VOLUME II : DRAMATIC SOPRANO

Laudate pueri (*113th Psalm*). Break my heart! (*Second Passion*). O magnify the Lord (*Chandos Anthem*). O King of Kings (*Esther*). In Jehova's awful sight (*Deborah*). My vengeance (*Athalia*). Come, pensive nun (*Il Pensieroso*). Vain fluctuating state (*Belshazzar*). Prophetic visions (*Occasional Oratorio*). With thee (*Solomon*). Guilt trembling (*Susanna*). See, Hercules (*The Choice of Hercules*).

VOLUME III : MEZZO-SOPRANO

Hope, thou pure and dearest treasure (*Esther*). O dreadful oracle (*Hercules*). Subtle love (*Alexander Balus*). What means this weight? (*Susanna*). Haste to the cedar grove (*Solomon*). O thou bright sun (*Theodora*). Dryads, Sylvans (*Time and Truth*).

VOLUME IV : CONTRALTO

Pleasure's gentle zephyrs (*Time and Truth*). Guards, seize the traitor (*Esther*). Impious mortal (*Deborah*). Then long eternity (*Samson*). She weeps (*Semele*). Great God (*Belshazzar*). See with what sad dejection (*Hercules*). Gold now is common (*Solomon*). Frost nips the flowers (*Susanna*). O bright example (*Theodora*). Yet can I hear (*The Choice of Hercules*).

VOLUME V : TENOR

Beatus vir (*Nisi Dominus*). Though bound (*Second Passion*). God is a constant sure defence (*Chandos Anthem*). Who dares (*Esther*). Would you gain (*Acis and Galathea*). The mighty master (*Alexander's Feast*). Great Dagon (*Samson*). Let the deep bowl (*Belshazzar*). Despair not (*Hercules*). O Lord, how many are my foes (*Occasional Oratorio*). To God who made the radiant sun (*Alexander Balus*). So long the memory (*Joshua*). From morn to eve (*Solomon*). Ye verdant hills (*Susanna*). Blessed are they (*Foundling Hospital Anthem*). Enjoy the sweet Elysian grove (*Alcesto*). Horror! Confusion! (*Jephta*). Pensive sorrow (*Time and Truth*).

VOLUME VI : BARITONE

O work sublime (*First Passion*). Ha! What vision (*La Resurrezione*). That God is great (*Chandos Anthem*). Turn not (*Esther*). Mountains on whose barren breast (*L'Allegro*). O Memory (*Belshazzar*). Oh Jove! (*Hercules*). To God our strength (*Occasional Oratorio*). And thus let happy Egypt's king (*Alexander Balus*). 'Tis Diocletian's natal day (*Theodora*). Ye fleeting shades (*Alceste*). Let me congratulate (*Jephta*). You hoped to call in vain (*Time and Truth*).

VOLUME VII : BASS

Ye heavens (*Second Passion*). O praise the Lord (*Chandos Anthem*). When storms the proud (*Athalia*). A serpent in my bosom (*Saul*). Vouchsafe, o Lord (*Dettingen Te Deum*). Since the race of time (*Joseph*). Leave me (*Semele*). Alcides' name (*Hercules*). To power immortal (*Belshazzar*). Why do the gentiles tumult (*Occasional Oratorio*). Great Prince (*Solomon*). Peace crowned (*Susanna*). Wide spread his name (*Theodora*). Like the shadow (*Time and Truth*).

The above-mentioned titles are not comprehensive to each volume.
For the complete contents consult the catalogue of Albums, Song Cycles, etc.

Boosey & Hawkes

Limited
295 Regent Street, London, W.1
Paris · Bonn · Capetown · Sydney · Toronto · New York

No. 602

6.51

Covent Garden Operas

A new series of booklets, attractively produced and illustrated, introducing Opera to the post-war generation. The background of each work is described and its musical characteristics are examined and explained, with the help of numerous quotations from the score.

Bizet .... **Carmen** .... Martin Cooper
Britten .... **Peter Grimes** ....Charles Stuart
Britten .... **The Rape of Lucretia**⎫ ....Hans Keller
                            Albert Herring ⎭
Massenet .... **Manon** .... Percy Colson
Mozart .... **The Magic Flute** ....Rupert Lee
Mussorgsky .... **Boris Godunov** .... Gerald Abraham
Strauss R. .... **Der Rosenkavalier** .... Alan Pryce-Jones
Verdi .... **Rigoletto** ..../............ F. Bonavia
Verdi .... **La Traviata** .... Trevor Fisher
Verdi .... **Il Trovatore** .... Dyneley Hussey
Wagner .... **Lohengrin** .... Hans Redlich
Wagner .... **The Mastersingers** .... Egon Wellesz
Wagner .... **The Rhinegold** ....Berta Geissmar
Wagner .... **The Valkyrie** .... Berta Geissmar
Wagner .... **Siegfried** .... Berta Geissmar
Wagner .... **The Twilight of the Gods** ..... Berta Geissmar
Wagner .... **Tristan and Isolde** .... Hans Redlich

Price 3/- each
(1952)

Tempo

An International Review of Modern Music
Published in Spring, Summer, Autumn and Winter
Annual Subscription: 8s. 8d. inc. postage ; Single copy, 2s. 2d. post free

Boosey & Hawkes

Limited

295 Regent Street, London, W.1

London · New York · Toronto · Sydney · Capetown · Buenos Aires · Paris · Bonn

No. 576

6.50